MW00928089

THIS BOOK BELONGS TO:

____

Made in the USA
Monee, IL
13 April 2023

31801090R00068